PRESIDENTS OF THE U.S.A.

ULYSSES S. GRANT

OUR EIGHTEENTH PRESIDENT

by Ann Graham Gaines

THE CHILD'S WORLD ®

Published in the United States of America

The Child's World®
1980 Lookout Drive • Mankato, MN 56003-1705
800-599-READ • www.childsworld.com

Acknowledgments
The Child's World®: Mary Berendes, Publishing Director

The Creative Spark: Mary McGavic, Project Director; Shari Joffe, Editorial
Director; Deborah Goodsite, Photo Research; Nancy Ratkiewich, Page Production

The Design Lab: Kathleen Petelinsek, Design

Content Adviser: Pam Sanfilippo, Historian, Ulysses S. Grant National Historic
Site, St. Louis, Missouri

Photos
Cover and page 3: White House Historical Association (White House Collection)
(detail); White House Historical Association (White House Collection)

Interior: The Art Archive: 17 and 39, 27 (Culver Pictures), 21 (National
Archives Washington D.C.); Art Resource, NY: 7, 22 (National Portrait Gallery,
Smithsonian Institution); The Bridgeman Art Library: 16 (Private Collection,
Peter Newark Military Pictures), 34 (Private Collection, Peter Newark American
Pictures); The Chicago History Museum: 11; Corbis: 4, 5, 25; The Granger
Collection, New York: 8, 13, 14 and 39, 32, 37; The Image Works: 18 (The
Print Collector/Heritage-Images), 23 (Topham), 28 , 30 (Mary Evans Picture
Library); iStockphoto: 44 (Tim Fan); Jupiter Images: 12 and 38 (Lindy Powers
/Index Stock); Keya Morgan, Lincoln Images.com, New York City: 20; Library
of Congress: 35, 36; North Wind Picture Archives: 29, 33 (North Wind); Ohio
Historical Society: 6; SuperStock: 19 (SuperStock, Inc); U.S. Air Force photo: 45.

Library of Congress Cataloging-in-Publication Data
Gaines, Ann.
  Ulysses S. Grant / by Ann Graham Gaines.
    p. cm. — (Presidents of the U.S.A.)
  Includes bibliographical references and index.
  ISBN 978-1-60253-047-8 (library bound : alk. paper)
  1. Grant, Ulysses S. (Ulysses Simpson), 1822–1885—Juvenile literature.
  2. Presidents—United States—Biography—Juvenile literature. 3. Generals—
  United States—Biography—Juvenile literature. I. Title.
  E672.G18 2008
  973.7'3092—dc22
  [B]
                              2007049065

Ulysses S. Grant, the greatest hero of the Civil War, became president of the United States in 1869.

TABLE OF CONTENTS

THE BEGINNING

Ulysses S. Grant was the 18th president of the United States. When he was elected to office in 1868, it was a difficult time for the nation. The Civil War had ended just three years earlier. Grant had been the general in charge of the **Union** army, which won the war over the **Confederacy.** Americans elected him in hopes that he could help heal the nation.

Grant was born in Point Pleasant, Ohio, on April 27, 1822. His parents, Hannah and Jesse, named him Hiram Ulysses Grant, but always called him Ulysses. Years later, when Grant arrived at West Point to attend the U.S. Military Academy, the school incorrectly had him listed as Ulysses S. Grant. From then on, he went by that name.

Grant's parents owned a small farm in Point Pleasant. They raised horses, pigs, and cows and also

Ulysses S. Grant is best known as an outstanding general who led the Northern states to victory during the Civil War.

grew vegetables and fruit. Jesse Grant had another job, too. He was a tanner, someone who makes animal skins or hides into leather. When Ulysses was born, his father worked in another tanner's shop.

When their son was just one year old, the Grants moved to the nearby town of Georgetown, Ohio. There they started a new farm. Jesse also opened a tannery of his own. Over time, he sold so many hides that he became a rich man.

As a child, Ulysses worked in his father's tannery. He hated the work. It was very messy and the hides smelled awful. When Jesse discovered that his son was good at working with horses, he let the boy do that instead. Ulysses hitched up horses and plowed the family's fields. He also drove the family's wagon. By the age of eight he was making deliveries for his father.

The first book Ulysses S. Grant ever read was a biography of George Washington.

After the Grants moved to Georgetown, Jesse opened a tannery (right). He often asked his sons to help him there, but Ulysses would do almost anything to avoid it. "He would rather do anything else under the sun than work in the tannery," Jesse once said of his son.

Ulysses S. Grant is said to have never forgotten a person's name.

When Ulysses was a boy, neighbors hired him to train their horses. His love for horses lasted throughout his life.

Ulysses was always very smart. Friends later remembered that he was a slow reader but had an amazing memory. As a small boy, he went to a one-room schoolhouse in Georgetown. He liked to read and was very good at math. By 14, he had learned all he could at the tiny school, so he went away to study, first at a private school in Kentucky and then at another school in Ohio. Soon he had completed his high-school education.

Ulysses did not think he wanted a career in the army. He went to the United States Military Academy at West Point to please his father. At West Point, he was an average student. The school offered regular college classes in subjects such as literature and mathematics. Its students mainly studied military subjects, such as military **strategy.** Outside of the classroom, students learned to march and handle weapons properly.

In 1843, Ulysses S. Grant graduated from West Point. At the time, he planned to spend just a few years in the army. His goal for the future was to become a math teacher. But first, like all other West Point graduates, he became an army **officer.**

The army first sent Grant to a fort in Missouri. There he met a young woman named Julia Boggs Dent. They secretly became engaged to be married. In 1844 he had to leave her when his **regiment** was sent to Louisiana.

Soon Grant's regiment transferred again, this time to Texas. War was about to break out between the United States and Mexico. When the Mexican War began in April 1846, Grant's regiment was sent to Mexico. There he fought in many battles. He became well known for his bravery and was **promoted** to the rank of first lieutenant. When the Americans captured the Mexican capital, Mexico City, the war ended. A **treaty** was signed in which Mexico gave the United States what would become the states of Texas, California, Nevada, Utah, and parts of Arizona, New Mexico, Colorado, and Wyoming.

At West Point Ulysses set a high-jump record that no one beat for more than 25 years.

This is the earliest known photograph of Ulysses S. Grant. It was taken shortly after he graduated from West Point, when he was a second lieutenant in the infantry.

The 1847 Battle of Vera Cruz (above) was among the battles Grant took part in during the Mexican War.

Some sources say Grant's middle name was Simpson, his mother's maiden name. That is not true. Grant never chose a middle name to go with the "S."

In 1848, Grant went back to Missouri. There he married Julia Dent. As a wedding present, Julia's parents gave the couple land near St. Louis. Grant stayed in the army, and Julia became an army wife. For a time, the couple lived at an army post in Michigan. Then they were sent to New York. In 1850, Julia gave birth to their first child, a son named Frederick.

In 1852, Grant was transferred to California. This time, Julia did not move with her husband. Instead, she stayed in Missouri with her relatives. While her husband was away, she gave birth to their second son.

JULIA DENT GRANT

Growing up, Julia Dent never dreamed she would one day become first lady of the United States.

Julia's father was a businessman. He moved his family from the East to St. Louis, Missouri. Julia was born there in 1826. Life in Missouri was not hard for the Dents. They owned a home in the city and a large farm in the country. They owned slaves who cooked, worked in their fields, and kept their house clean.

Julia received a fine education for a girl of her day. In 1843, at age 17, she graduated from a private school. The next year she met Ulysses Grant. Julia's brother had attended West Point. Grant was one of his classmates. After Grant graduated from West Point, he was assigned to a military post in St. Louis. He then went to visit Julia's brother. The Dents often invited Grant back. He and Julia soon fell in love. They did not marry, however, for four years, until Grant finished fighting in the Mexican War.

The early years of their marriage were difficult for Julia. Her husband's army career moved the family often, and the pay was low. In eight years, she had four children. She did not like it when she had to be separated from her husband. During the Civil War, she constantly feared for her husband's life. But through good times and bad, Grant was always a devoted husband and father. "Since I have loved Julia, I have loved no one else," he once wrote. Theirs was a strong, happy marriage. In fact, their four children agreed that they never heard a cross word spoken between them.

CIVIL WAR

Ulysses S. Grant served in the U.S. Army two times. The first time was for eleven years, from his graduation from West Point in 1843 until 1854. For most of that time, he did well in the army, gaining a good reputation. But when he was transferred to California, he missed his wife and family, and was lonely and depressed. Finally, in 1854, he resigned from the army and was reunited with his family.

Grant was happy to leave California to return to his beloved family. But the next ten years would prove hard. In St. Louis, he built a four-room log cabin on the land he and Julia had received as a wedding present. He farmed both their land and land belonging to Julia's father. Because of an economic **depression** and bad weather, he didn't make enough money farming, so he also started to buy and sell land. But he didn't succeed in real estate either. In 1860, the family moved to Galena, Illinois, so that Ulysses could go to work in a hardware and leather store owned by his father and run by his two brothers.

Just 11 months later, the Civil War began. Eleven Southern states had **seceded**—withdrawn—from the

During the Civil War, Ulysses S. Grant developed a terrible smoking habit. He sometimes smoked 20 cigars a day. This would later cause him to get throat cancer.

Before the start of the Civil War, Grant worked at his family's hardware and leather goods store in Galena, Illinois.

Union and formed their own country. They called it the Confederate States of America. When President Lincoln took office, he decided it was worth going to war to bring the Southern states back into the Union. Grant agreed with Lincoln. In 1861, he left his job at the hardware store and enlisted in the U.S. Army for a second time.

General Grant is shown here about to mount his horse during the Civil War. General Grant was an excellent horseman. Even as a small boy, he had a special gift for relating to horses. He was allowed to play alone in his father's horse stall under the bellies of the horses, and they never harmed him. His mother once said, "Horses seem to understand Ulysses."

Grant missed his family very much whenever he was away. In fact, during the war, Julia and his children visited him at his army camp whenever possible.

In June 1861, the governor of Illinois made Grant the commander of a regiment of volunteers—other men who had just signed up for the army. Most of Grant's men were young and had little experience, but he trained them well and they became excellent soldiers. Grant impressed his commanders so much that President Lincoln promoted him to brigadier general in July.

For a time, Grant's troops remained west of the action, camped first in Missouri and then Illinois. In September, they crossed the river into Kentucky. Confederate soldiers had occupied the city of Columbus. Grant forced them to leave. Then he convinced his superiors to let him to take his men to Tennessee. There they forced Confederate soldiers to abandon first Fort Henry and then Fort Donelson. The **surrender** of Fort Donelson on February 16, 1862, was the first major Union victory of the war. Fifteen thousand Confederates surrendered to Grant. President Abraham Lincoln rejoiced at the news. He praised Grant and promoted him to major general. Grant became a national hero.

After these victories, Grant remained with his troops in Tennessee. By this time, he had 42,000 men under his command. He began to make preparations to attack a Confederate rail center just a few miles away in Mississippi. But in early April, Confederate soldiers surprised Grant. Confederate General Albert Sidney Johnston had been laying his own plans, to attack Grant's troops. The Confederates attacked Union troops camped at the Shiloh Church on April 6.

After Grant's victory at Fort Donelson, Americans nicknamed him "Unconditional Surrender." This was because he demanded complete and unconditional surrender from the Confederate forces at the battle.

General Grant's army invaded western Tennessee in 1862. After Union soldiers defeated the Confederates at Fort Donelson (below), the Union took control of western Tennessee and Nashville. This was Grant's and the Union's first major success during the war.

The Confederates launched a surprise attack on Grant's forces at the 1862 Battle of Shiloh. Though the Union forces were unprepared, they managed to hold their own, and on the second day of battle, the Confederates were forced to retreat. Still, the great loss of life on both sides showed Grant and other leaders that the Civil War was not likely to end quickly.

Julia was once nearly captured by the Confederates during the Civil War. They arrived at the house where she had stayed the day before, but she had left to join her husband.

From his headquarters nearby, Grant could hear the sounds of fighting. He rushed to take part in what would become known as the Battle of Shiloh. Grant displayed great courage there. His fierce fighting inspired his men to fight hard, too.

The Battle of Shiloh continued for two days. The Confederates finally retreated. The Union counted the battle as a victory. But both sides had suffered terrible losses. Thousands of Union and Confederate soldiers had died or been wounded at Shiloh. The battle made people on both sides realize that this was going to be a terrible war.

After the battle, many people criticized Ulysses S. Grant for having been surprised by the Confederates. Some Union army officials wanted President Lincoln to fire Grant. But Lincoln refused to do so. He explained, "I can't spare this man. He fights."

In the summer of 1862, Abraham Lincoln put Grant in command of thousands more men. That fall, Grant began laying plans to take the city of Vicksburg, Mississippi. Vicksburg was a place of great importance to the Confederates. As long as their soldiers controlled it, they could ship goods up and down the Mississippi River. It also allowed them to communicate quickly by sending messengers up the river.

Grant was determined to take Vicksburg. It would take him months to do so. Finally, however, he succeeded. The Confederates at Vicksburg surrendered to Grant on July 4, 1863. Grant took 20,000 Confederate soldiers prisoner. This victory split the Confederate States of America in two because it could no longer use the Mississippi River. Losing access to the river made it difficult for the Confederate government and its army to function.

After Vicksburg, Grant was named a major general. His next big challenge was to fight the Confederates at Chattanooga, Tennessee. There another Union general, William S. Rosencras, and his Army of the Cumberland, had been nearly surrounded

Grant's son Fred also spent time with his father during the Civil War. Fred was wounded when a musket ball struck him in the left thigh at the Battle of Black River Bridge. He was thirteen years old.

For every soldier killed in battle during the Civil War, two died of disease.

Grant was very thin during the war, weighing only 135 pounds.

15

Grant's victory at Vicksburg gave Union forces control of the Mississippi River.

Six future presidents fought on the side of the North during the Civil War: Ulysses S. Grant, Chester A. Arthur, James A. Garfield, Benjamin Harrison, Rutherford B. Hayes, and William McKinley.

by Confederates. In November 1863, Grant used his own men to force the Confederates to retreat. After that victory, Lincoln promoted him yet again, putting him in charge of the entire Union army.

Grant made plans for the rest of the war. He ordered General William Tecumseh Sherman to fight through the South. At the same time, Grant battled Confederate General Robert E. Lee's Army of Northern Virginia. The soldiers on both sides fought very hard. Nevertheless, bit by bit, Grant wore down General Lee and his men.

GRANT AND LINCOLN

During the Civil War, Ulysses S. Grant and Abraham Lincoln developed a great loyalty to and respect for one another. At the beginning of the war, Abraham Lincoln had few generals upon whom he could depend. He knew little about Ulysses Grant until the Confederates in Vicksburg, Mississippi, surrendered. Lincoln then realized that Grant was a great leader, a man he could count on to fight to the end. After Lincoln put Grant in charge of all Union armies, the United States began to defeat the Confederate States of America.

Lincoln and Grant met several times during the war. Grant visited Lincoln in the White House to discuss war plans. Lincoln visited Grant's camp on the battlefield. They were both quiet, thoughtful men who listened to one another. As the North came closer to victory, Americans thanked both the great general and the president for saving the Union.

General Grant (second from left) meeting with President Lincoln (hand on chin).

C H A P T E R T H R E E
★★★★★★★★★★★★★★★★★★★

AFTER THE WAR

By April of 1865, the end of the Civil War was near. Both sides continued to fight bravely, but Grant's strategy kept the Confederates on the defensive and wore them down. Grant was finally able to surround Confederate General Robert E. Lee's army. There was no escape. Lee had no choice but to give in.

The two generals arranged to meet at Appomattox Courthouse in Virginia on the morning of April 9, 1865, so Lee could surrender to Grant. Lee had been afraid that thousands of Confederate soldiers might be tried for **treason** and hung. But Grant simply required them to lay down their arms and promise to fight no more.

President Lincoln was pleased with the terms Grant offered. He wanted to see the South treated in a kind and fair way. However, other Americans thought Grant had not punished the

By the end of the Civil War, General Grant was considered a great hero.

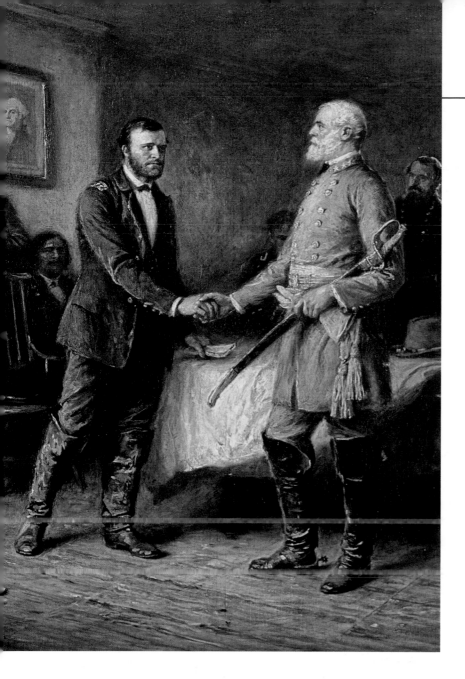

Confederate General Robert E. Lee surrendered to Grant on April 9, 1865. Grant later wrote about the event: "I said to Lee that I hoped and believed this would be the close of the war; that it was most important that the men should go home and go to work."

In April of 1865, after the surrender at Appomattox, Grant reported to Lincoln in Washington, D.C. Lincoln invited him to stay and go to the theater with him one night. Grant refused. He wanted very much to see his family who were then living in New Jersey. Had Grant accepted, he would have been in Ford's Theater the night that John Wilkes Booth **assassinated** President Lincoln.

Confederates severely enough. Many people believed the South was to blame for the terrible war. After all, they had rebelled against the Union.

The Civil War continued for a short time after Lee's surrender. Union General Sherman accepted Confederate General Johnston's surrender on the same

Grant had lived in Galena for only a year before the Civil War began. Few people knew him at the time, but by the end of the war, he was famous. Cheering citizens greeted him upon his return.

terms that Grant had offered Lee. This ended fighting in the South. Confederate President Jefferson Davis was soon captured. There were a few more small battles in the west, but the last Confederate soldiers laid down their arms on June 23, 1865.

Historians have described the Civil War as the bloodiest war in the history of the United States. More than three million men had fought in the war. Around 600,000 soldiers died. That number included 350,000 Northerners and 250,000 Southerners. Cities and towns in the North had suffered little damage during the war because few battles had taken place there. But there had been many battles in the South, and much of it lay in ruins. Union soldiers had taken Southern farmers' crops and equipment. Abraham Lincoln had declared all Southern slaves free during the war, and many slaves had left their owners. When the Civil War ended, slave owners had to release the people whom they still held in bondage.

The term **Reconstruction** is used to describe the period during which the Union was restored. Lincoln had wanted to make the South's return to the Union

Julia Grant's family owned slaves. In fact, her father once gave Ulysses Grant a slave named William Jones. Grant could have made money by selling Jones. Instead, he signed a document that gave Jones his freedom.

After the war, much of the South, including Richmond, Virginia (left), was in ruins. Men, women, and children in every Southern state were starving. People's homes and other buildings were destroyed. Now Union leaders had to decide how much help to give these states that most Northerners blamed for starting the war.

The end of the war meant Grant had more time to spend with his family, whom he loved deeply. One of Grant's friends remembered seeing the family together during the war. "The children often romped with him and he joined in their frolics. . . . The younger ones would hang around his neck while he was writing, make a terrible mess of the papers, and turn everything in his tent into a toy."

as easy as possible. He thought Southerners loyal to the Union should be allowed to decide many matters for themselves. One thing he believed was that the Southern states should be allowed to write their own new state **constitutions,** as long as they included freedom for blacks.

Some members of Lincoln's **political party,** the Republicans, thought the South deserved to be punished. These men called themselves the Radical Republicans. They did not want former Confederates to be allowed to hold any political office. They also wanted the former slaves to be granted **civil rights** at once. These views became popular with many people in the North.

On April 14, 1865, Abraham Lincoln was shot by an assassin. He died the next day. Vice President Andrew Johnson became president. Johnson had been born in the South, in North Carolina, but he never supported the states that had seceded from the Union. He had always remained loyal to the United States. Once the war was over, however, he wanted to help the South. He had different ideas than Lincoln and the Radical Republicans. He did not believe that

President Andrew Johnson was a Southerner, and he wanted to help the South rebuild itself after the war. But many members of Congress wanted to punish the Confederates. They could not agree with Johnson about how to go about the process of Reconstruction. In the end, Johnson was an unpopular president.

As a young man, Grant had no interest in **politics**. He never dreamed of holding any public office. By 1868, he had changed his mind. Many people felt that Grant was the only person who could reunite the nation after the Civil War.

The 13th Amendment abolished slavery in the United States. It was ratified in December 1865.

any African Americans deserved the same rights as white people. Johnson was a member of the Democratic Party, which had ideas very different from those of the Republicans. From the start, Johnson fought fiercely against the Radical Republicans in Congress.

In 1866, Radical Republicans persuaded Congress to pass the 14th **Amendment** to the U.S. Constitution. This granted civil rights to all persons born in the United States. It also said no state could take away these rights. To President Johnson's dismay, blacks were finally recognized as citizens. Congress decided only Southern states that **ratified,** or approved, the 13th and 14th amendments would be readmitted to the Union. In 1867, Congress passed the Reconstruction Act. This law put the U.S. military in charge of Southern states until they were readmitted to the Union.

During this period, Ulysses Grant remained in the army. He toured the South on behalf of the government, talking about Reconstruction. Grant did not think the South should be punished harshly. He wanted to see it become strong and stable once more, believing it was the only way to restore the Union. Still, Grant did differ with many Southerners—and President Johnson—on one point. He fully supported equal rights for blacks, including giving black men the right to vote. (At the time, no women in the United States were allowed to vote.)

In 1867, Grant also served as secretary of war, an advisor to the president, for a short time. He replaced

OUR COUNTRY'S HEROES.

Voters had high hopes that Grant would be a strong president because of his record during the Civil War. This print groups Grant with two of America's greatest heroes: George Washington and Abraham Lincoln.

Edwin M. Stanton, whom President Johnson had fired. Congress later gave back Stanton's job, saying he had been unfairly dismissed. Grant stepped down from his position without complaint. His decision to leave peacefully, without making a fuss, made President Johnson angry. Johnson wanted Grant to insist that the job was his.

At his inauguration, Grant said he hoped to renew a spirit of goodwill among all people in the United States. He knew the reconstruction of the South would be the most important issue of his term.

When it was time for another election, most people did not want Andrew Johnson to run for president. His party, the Democrats, chose another man as their **candidate.** Ulysses S. Grant had become a hero to the American people during the Civil War. He was still extremely popular. The Republicans hoped they could convince Grant to run for office. In 1868, the Republican Party chose Grant as its presidential candidate, and he won the election that November. He was **inaugurated** in March of 1869.

CHAPTER FOUR

THE PRESIDENCY

Ulysses S. Grant had been a very successful general, but he faced great challenges as president. Among those challenges were the **scandals** that plagued his presidency and hurt his reputation.

He had one very big problem: although he was an honest man, many people close to him were not. During President Grant's first year in office, he became friends with two men, James Fisk and Jay Gould. He did not know they planned to corner the gold market—to control its sale everywhere in the United States so they could control its price. Their plan was illegal. Grant figured out their plan and knew he had to stop it. He ordered that $4 million of government gold be put on the market and sold. Unfortunately, this

President Grant, an honest man, made the mistake of trusting people who turned out to be dishonest.

greatly lowered the price of gold. People who owned it lost a great deal of money, but President Grant's actions saved the country from financial disaster.

The president turned his attention to the most important issue of the day: Reconstruction. One of his main goals was to help black Americans. As a general, Grant had trained and commanded black soldiers. He had helped slaves gain their freedom. As president, he hoped to ensure that they would gain equal rights.

During his presidency, he fought for African Americans' rights. One thing he did was to push Congress to pass the 15th Amendment. This 1870

This print shows angry citizens mobbing the New York offices of Jay Gould and James Fisk. The two men, who were friends of Grant's, were involved in a gold scandal that caused a financial crisis during Grant's presidency.

addition to the Constitution guaranteed black men the right to vote. Some black men had voted in the previous election, but this amendment promised that this right could never be taken away. Grant also got Congress to pass the Enforcement Act of 1870, which said the government could send its troops to the South if anyone tried to stop black men from voting.

Another bill that Grant supported was the Ku Klux Klan Act of 1871. The Ku Klux Klan was a group of Southern white men that used violence— beatings, whippings, and even murder—to control blacks. Local governments and police wouldn't do anything to stop this. In fact, some leaders and police were even members of the Klan. The Ku Klux Klan

When Grant became
president, there
were 37 states in
the Union. Colorado
became a state during
his presidency.

Julia Grant earned
a reputation as a
great hostess in
Washington, D.C. Her
fancy parties were
described as "galas."

Even after slavery was made illegal, life for African Americans in the South was difficult. Many, like the people shown in this photograph, worked on the same farms as they had when they were slaves, earning barely enough money to survive. President Grant did what he could to help them, but his efforts accomplished little.

Act said troops could be sent to the South to stop the Klan. Unfortunately, this was effective only as long as the troops stayed in the South. As soon as they left, blacks were again victims of violence and hatred.

Grant tried hard to convince Americans that Southern white men who had supported the Confederacy should not have total control of their state governments. Unfortunately, he failed. The laws passed by Congress were not enough. White men continued to have all the political power in the South. They controlled the Southern states' governments. These governments passed laws known as the Black Codes. These laws prevented blacks from living as fully free people. They made sure that blacks remained poor and landless. To Ulysses S. Grant's sadness, in the South, the lives of former slaves were little better than they had been during the time of slavery.

In 1871, Grant was able to celebrate an achievement. The United States signed the Treaty of Washington with Great Britain, which required the British to pay the United States $15 million. This was to pay for damage the Confederates, using ships built in Britain, had done to the Union during the Civil War. President Grant also settled the border with Canada, and kept the United States out of war with Cuba. He supported efforts for the United States to grow bigger. He wanted the United States to take over Santo Domingo on the Caribbean island of Hispaniola. He thought this would increase American trade in the Caribbean Sea. He also thought Southern blacks might want to settle there. But Congress rejected the treaty. The United States did not take over Santo Domingo. Today it is the nation of the Dominican Republic.

In 1872, more scandals surfaced. Some of Grant's closest advisors were involved. The worst involved the transcontinental railroad. Building this coast-to-coast railroad cost the federal government nearly $3 billion. The owners of a construction company called Crédit Mobilier of America wanted to keep some of the money for themselves. They overcharged the government for work the company did on the transcontinental railroad. Then they stole the money.

Unfortunately, Grant's vice president, Schuyler Colfax, was accused of accepting money from Crédit Mobilier. With the election of 1872 drawing near, Grant had to choose a new vice presidential candidate.

During Grant's presidency, his daughter, Nellie, was married in a ceremony at the White House.

While president, Ulysses S. Grant was once arrested for speeding in Washington, D.C. He was driving his horses too fast and was fined $20.

Even with all these problems, the American people believed that Grant was an honest man. In the election of 1872, Grant won a second term of office. His new vice president was Henry Wilson.

Throughout Grant's presidency, the nation had money problems. For one thing, the government was still paying for the Civil War. Grant reduced the size of the army and made sure that the national debt was

Despite the troubles of Grant's first term, voters believed that Grant was a decent, upstanding man who deserved a second term. This 1872 campaign poster portrays Grant as a hardworking tanner—just like his father was. His new choice for vice president, Henry Wilson, is shown as a strong, competent shoemaker.

THE WORKING MAN'S BANNER.

FOR PRESIDENT. FOR VICE-PRESIDENT.

TANNERY

ULYSSES S. GRANT
"The Galena Tanner"

HENRY WILSON
"The Natick Shoemaker"

Grant's second term brought even more problems. In 1873, there was a financial panic (left). Many banks closed, and the nation sank into a five-year-long depression.

paid down as quickly as possible. But in addition, the massive railroad project was draining funds from both the government and from private sources. Things grew more serious during Grant's second term. In the fall of 1873, many banks went out of business. Soon many small companies were forced to close as well. A depression began that lasted for five years. Millions of Americans lost their jobs.

As the nation suffered through the depression, the public learned of more scandals in the government. The secretary of the treasury, William Richardson, placed a close friend in charge of collecting overdue **taxes.** Richardson made a deal that allowed his friend to keep half of what he collected for himself. By the time anyone found out, the tax agent had pocketed $200,000.

Other problems surfaced as well. Grant's personal secretary and many revenue agents were accused of accepting **bribes** from liquor companies that did not

Alexander Graham Bell invented the telephone during Grant's presidency.

Let us have a piece.

Let us have a piece.

Let us have peace.

Let us have a piece.

GOVERNMENT CAKE.

A NICE FAMILY PARTY.

want to pay whiskey taxes. This type of thing had been going on for years, but Grant finally did something about it. His insistence that "no guilty man escape" led to over 350 **indictments** throughout the country. Also, Grant's secretary of war was involved in the illegal sale of Native American trading posts. While these government workers and businessmen were using their power to get richer, the rest of the nation was still suffering through the terrible depression.

Ulysses S. Grant's second term was very hard on him. He was very embarrassed and angered by the wrongdoings of men he had appointed to his cabinet. He had very few moments when he felt proud. One must have been when Congress passed the Civil Rights Act of 1875. That law said that whites could no longer keep blacks out of public places, such as hotels, restaurants, and theaters. Unfortunately, this law had little effect because it proved difficult to enforce. In 1883, six years after Grant left office, the Supreme Court decided it went against the laws of the U.S. Constitution.

Grant left office in 1877, disappointed that he had not been able to achieve everything he had hoped to achieve. He and Julia went on a round-the-world tour that lasted more than two years. By the time Grant arrived back home, he was popular once again. In 1880, many Republicans hoped Grant would run for president a third time. After 35 **ballots,** Republicans instead chose James A. Garfield as their candidate.

After that, Grant and his wife moved to New York City. He invested in various businesses. In 1884, one firm in which he had invested went out of business. Grant had huge debts. He worried about how to provide for his family. He took the advice of his close friend, the famous author Mark Twain, who suggested that Grant write his **memoirs** to earn money. Twain believed many people would want to read about Grant's life as a military leader and politician.

Grant's memoirs became a bestseller, among the most-read books of the day. The Grant family made $500,000 from its sale.

The Grants traveled the world after Grant's second term ended. They are shown here (seated third and fourth from left) at a temple in Luxor, Egypt.

35

Grant's bad luck continued, however. Just as he began writing his book, tragedy struck. One day while eating a piece of fruit, he felt terrible pain. After being examined by his doctor, Grant learned that he had cancer of the throat caused by his lifetime habit of smoking cigars.

Grant's health grew weaker, but he was determined to finish his memoirs. He completed his work in the summer of 1885. He died on July 23, just one week after putting down his pen. Americans mourned his death and honored his heroism during the Civil War. Today he is remembered as a great general who helped to restore the Union in a time of crisis, and as a president who worked hard to reunite the nation and ensure equality for all.

It was Mark Twain who published Grant's memoirs.

Grant's health grew steadily worse after he learned he had throat cancer. As he struggled to finish his memoirs, he often felt too sick to do anything else. "There cannot be a hope of going far beyond this time," he said. "It is nearly impossible for me to swallow. It pains me even to talk."

THE 15ᵀᴴ AMENDMENT

During Reconstruction, Southern states were forced to permit black men to vote. But many Northern states still denied them the right. In 1869, Congress voted in favor of the 15th Amendment to the U.S. Constitution. It stated that suffrage (the right to vote) could not be denied because of race, color, or "previous condition of servitude." The amendment became law in March of 1870. Four Southern states had ratified the amendment only because they would not have been permitted to rejoin the Union otherwise.

Even after the amendment was passed, black men continued to be denied the right to vote. This was because some states passed laws stating that men had to own property or pass a literacy test to be able to vote. In other places, blacks were threatened with violence if they attempted to vote. The 15th Amendment did not prohibit such voting restrictions. It also did not extend the right to vote to black women. At that time, no women were allowed to vote in the United States. Women had already begun to fight for the right, but they would have to continue to do so for years. The 19th Amendment, which gave women the right to vote, was finally approved in 1920. It wasn't until the Voting Rights Act of 1965 was passed that African Americans were fully guaranteed their right to vote in the United States.

Time Line

| 1820 | 1830 | 1840 | 1850 | 1860 |

1822
Ulysses S. Grant is born on April 27 in Point Pleasant, Ohio.

1828
At age 6, Grant starts school.

1839
Grant enrolls at the U.S. Military Academy, West Point, at age 17.

1843
Grant graduates from West Point at age 21.

1846
After being assigned to several different army posts, Grant fights in the Mexican War.

1848
The Mexican War ends. Grant travels to St. Louis, Missouri, where he marries his sweetheart, Julia Dent.

1852
The army stations Grant at a fort in California. He misses his family terribly.

1854
Grant resigns from the army. He returns to St. Louis and his family. They start a farm.

1860
Since leaving the army, Grant tries various jobs to provide for his family. He moves his family to Galena, Illinois, where he works in the hardware and leather store owned by his family.

1861
The Civil War begins. Grant joins the Union army.

1862
On February 6, Grant and the men under his command win a small battle at Fort Henry, Tennessee. Ten days later, they win the first major Union victory of the war. About 15,000 Confederate soldiers surrender to Grant at Fort Donelson on the Cumberland River in Tennessee. In April, Confederate troops surprise him at the Battle of Shiloh.

1863
Thousands of Confederate soldiers surrender to Grant after his siege of Vicksburg, Mississippi.

1864
Lincoln appoints Grant general in chief of the Union army.

1865
On April 9, Confederate general Robert E. Lee surrenders to Grant at Appomattox Courthouse in Virginia. President Lincoln is assassinated five days later. In December, the 13th Amendment is ratified, abolishing slavery in the United States.

1866
After the war, Grant is named general of the armies of the United States. Congress passes the 14th Amendment to the U.S. Constitution, granting civil rights to all persons born in the United States.

1867
Congress passes the Reconstruction Act, which puts the U.S. military in charge of Southern states. Grant is briefly President Johnson's secretary of war.

1868
The Republican political party nominates Grant as its presidential candidate. He wins the election.

1869
Grant is inaugurated as president of the United States. In May, the transcontinental railroad is completed. James Fisk and Jay Gould plan to corner the gold market with the aid of President Grant's brother-in-law. Grant learns of the plan and takes action to stop it. This is the first of many scandals during Grant's time in office.

1870
The 15th Amendment is ratified, giving black men the right to vote. The first Enforcement Act is passed, which allows the government to send troops to the South if anyone attempts to stop black men from voting.

1871
The Ku Klux Klan Act is passed, allowing the government to send troops to the South to stop the Klan from committing violent acts. The United States and Great Britain sign the Treaty of Washington.

1872
Grant's vice president is accused of taking bribes in the Crédit Mobilier scandal. The Republican Party must select a new vice presidential candidate, Henry Wilson, for the upcoming election. Grant is elected to a second term.

1873
A depression begins that lasts five years. Millions of Americans lose their jobs as companies go out of business.

1875
The Civil Rights Act says that whites cannot keep blacks out of public places, such as hotels, restaurants, and theaters. The law is not enforced in many places.

1877
Grant leaves office. He and his wife, Julia, depart on a round-the-world tour that lasts two years.

1880
Some Republicans encourage Grant to run for president again, but James Garfield is chosen to run as the Republican candidate instead.

1884
Grant starts to write his memoirs. He is diagnosed with cancer of the throat.

1885
Ulysses S. Grant completes his memoirs only a week before he dies on July 23. Mark Twain ensures that Grant's work is published. It becomes a bestseller.

GLOSSARY

amendment (uh-MEND-ment)) An amendment is a change or addition made to the Constitution or other documents. Congress passed the 14th Amendment in 1866.

assassinated (uh-SASS-ih-nay-tid) If someone assassinated another person, they murdered them. John Wilkes Booth assassinated President Lincoln in 1865.

ballots (BA-luts) A ballot is a round of voting. After 35 ballots, Republicans in 1880 chose James Garfield instead of Grant as their presidential candidate.

bribes (BRIBES) Bribes are gifts or money offered to a person in exchange for that person doing something for the offerer, especially something wrong. President Grant's personal secretary was accused of accepting bribes from companies that did not want to pay taxes.

candidate (KAN-dih-det) A candidate is a person running in an election. In 1868, the Republican Party chose Grant as its presidential candidate.

civil rights (SIH-vel RYTZ) Civil rights are the rights guaranteed by the Constitution to all citizens of the United States. Radical Republicans wanted blacks to have civil rights.

Confederacy (kuhn-FED-ur-uh-see) A confederacy is a union of states or people with a common goal. In American history, the Confederacy was a group of 11 states that declared its independence from the rest of the Union before the Civil War.

constitutions (con-stih-TOO-shuns) Constitutions are sets of basic principles that govern states, countries, or societies. The U.S. Constitution includes the principles that govern the United States.

depression (deh-PRESH-un) A depression is a period of time in which there is little business activity, and many people are out of work. A depression began in 1873 that lasted for five years.

inaugurated (ih-NAWG-yuh-rayt-id) When politicians are inaugurated, they formally enter an elected office. Grant was inaugurated the 18th president in 1869.

indictment (in-DITE-ment) When someone is given an indictment, they are officially charged with a crime. More than 350 indictments were handed down in the Whiskey Ring scandal during Grant's presidency.

memoirs (MEM-wahrz) Memoirs are a written account of a person's life. Grant wrote his memoirs in the last year of his life.

officer (AW-feh-ser) An officer is a leader in the military who commands other soldiers. Grant became an officer after graduating from West point.

political party (puh-LIT-ih-kul PAR-tee) A political party is a group of people who share similar ideas about how to run a government. Lincoln and Grant were both members of the Republican political party.

politics (PAWL-ih-tiks) Politics refers to the actions and practices of the government. Grant had no interest in politics as a young man.

promoted (pruh-MOH-tid) People who are promoted receive a more important job or position to recognize their good work. Grant was promoted in the army because of his excellent fighting during the war.

ratified (RAT-uh-fyed) Ratified means agreed or approved officially. Congress ratified the 14th Amendment in 1866.

Reconstruction (ree-kun-STRUK-shun) Reconstruction is the rebuilding of something. The period in history after the Civil War is known as Reconstruction because the nation was trying to rebuild the Union.

regiment (REJ-ih-ment) A regiment is a group of soldiers led by a colonel. Grant was part of a regiment that was sent to Mexico during the Mexican War.

scandals (SKAN-delz) Scandals are shameful private or public actions that shock the public. Scandals plagued Grant's presidency.

seceded (suh-SEED-id) If a group seceded, it separated from a larger group. The Southern states seceded from the Union in 1860 and 1861.

strategy (STRAT-eh-jee) In the military, strategy is the science of planning and directing movements and operations. Students at West Point study military strategy.

surrender (suh-REN-dur) If an army surrenders, it gives up to its enemy. A Confederate army of 15,000 soldiers surrendered to Grant at Fort Donelson.

taxes (TAK-sez) Taxes are sums of money that citizens pay to support their government. A scandal involving taxes occurred during Grant's presidency.

treason (TREE-zun) Treason is the act of hurting one's country or helping its enemies. General Lee worried that Confederate soldiers would be punished for treason.

treaty (TREE-tee) A treaty is a formal agreement between nations. The United States signed the Treaty of Washington with Great Britain in 1871.

Union (YOON-yen) The Union is another name for the United States. During the Civil War, the Northern states were called the Union.

THE UNITED STATES GOVERNMENT

The United States government is divided into three equal branches: the executive, the legislative, and the judicial. This division helps prevent abuses of power because each branch has to answer to the other two. No one branch can become too powerful.

EXECUTIVE BRANCH

President
Vice President
Departments

The job of the executive branch is to enforce the laws. It is headed by the president, who serves as the spokesperson for the United States around the world. The president signs bills into law and appoints important officials such as federal judges. He or she is also the commander in chief of the U.S. military. The president is assisted by the vice president, who takes over if the president dies or cannot carry out the duties of the office.

The executive branch also includes various departments, each focused on a specific topic. They include the Defense Department, the Justice Department, and the Agriculture Department. The department heads, along with other officials such as the vice president, serve as the president's closest advisers, called the cabinet.

LEGISLATIVE BRANCH

Congress
Senate and
House of Representatives

The job of the legislative branch is to make the laws. It consists of Congress, which is divided into two parts: the Senate and the House of Representatives. The Senate has 100 members, and the House of Representatives has 435 members. Each state has two senators. The number of representatives a state has varies depending on the state's population.

Besides making laws, Congress also passes budgets and enacts taxes. In addition, it is responsible for declaring war, maintaining the military, and regulating trade with other countries.

JUDICIAL BRANCH

Supreme Court
Courts of Appeals
District Courts

The job of the judicial branch is to interpret the laws. It consists of the nation's federal courts. Trials are held in district courts. During trials, judges must decide what laws mean and how they apply. Courts of appeals review the decisions made in district courts.

The nation's highest court is the Supreme Court. If someone disagrees with a court of appeals ruling, he or she can ask the Supreme Court to review it. The Supreme Court may refuse. The Supreme Court makes sure that decisions and laws do not violate the Constitution.

CHOOSING
THE PRESIDENT

It may seem odd, but American voters don't elect the president directly. Instead, the president is chosen using what is called the Electoral College.

Each state gets as many votes in the Electoral College as its combined total of senators and representatives in Congress. For example, Iowa has two senators and five representatives, so it gets seven electoral votes. Although the District of Columbia does not have any voting members in Congress, it gets three electoral votes. Usually, the candidate who wins the most votes in any given state receives all of that state's electoral votes.

To become president, a candidate must get more than half of the Electoral College votes. There are a total of 538 votes in the Electoral College, so a candidate needs 270 votes to win. If nobody receives 270 Electoral College votes, the House of Representatives chooses the president.

With the Electoral College system, the person who receives the most votes nationwide does not always receive the most electoral votes. This happened most recently in 2000, when Al Gore received half a million more national votes than George W. Bush. Bush became president because he had more Electoral College votes.

THE WHITE HOUSE

The White House is the official home of the president of the United States. It is located at 1600 Pennsylvania Avenue NW in Washington, D.C. In 1792, a contest was held to select the architect who would design the president's home. James Hoban won. Construction took eight years.

The first president, George Washington, never lived in the White House. The second president, John Adams, moved into the house in 1800, though the inside was not yet complete. During the War of 1812, British soldiers burned down much of the White House. It was rebuilt several years later.

The White House was changed through the years. Porches were added, and President Theodore Roosevelt added the West Wing. President William Taft changed the shape of the presidential office, making it into the famous Oval Office. While Harry Truman was president, the old house was discovered to be structurally weak. All the walls were reinforced with steel, and the rooms were rebuilt.

Today, the White House has 132 rooms (including 35 bathrooms), 28 fireplaces, and 3 elevators. It takes 570 gallons of paint to cover the outside of the six-story building. The White House provides the president with many ways to relax. It includes a putting green, a jogging track, a swimming pool, a tennis court, and beautifully landscaped gardens. The White House also has a movie theater, a billiard room, and a one-lane bowling alley.

PRESIDENTIAL PERKS

The job of president of the United States is challenging. It is probably one of the most stressful jobs in the world. Because of this, presidents are paid well, though not nearly as well as the leaders of large corporations. In 2007, the president earned $400,000 a year. Presidents also receive extra benefits that make the demanding job a little more appealing.

★ **Camp David:** In the 1940s, President Franklin D. Roosevelt chose this heavily wooded spot in the mountains of Maryland to be the presidential retreat, where presidents can relax. Even though it is a retreat, world business is conducted there. Most famously, President Jimmy Carter met with Middle Eastern leaders at Camp David in 1978. The result was a peace agreement between Israel and Egypt.

★ *Air Force One:* The president flies on a jet called *Air Force One*. It is a Boeing 747-200B that has been modified to meet the president's needs.

Air Force One is the size of a large home. It is equipped with a dining room, sleeping quarters, a conference room, and office space. It also has two kitchens that can provide food for up to 50 people.

★ **The Secret Service:** While not the most glamorous of the president's perks, the Secret Service is one of the most important. The Secret Service is a group of highly trained agents who protect the president and the president's family.

★ **The Presidential State Car:** The presidential limousine is a stretch Cadillac DTS.

It has been armored to protect the president in case of attack. Inside the plush car are a foldaway desk, an entertainment center, and a communications console.

★ **The Food:** The White House has five chefs who will make any food the president wants. The White House also has an extensive wine collection.

★ **Retirement:** A former president receives a pension, or retirement pay, of just under $180,000 a year. Former presidents also receive Secret Service protection for the rest of their lives.

F A C T S

QUALIFICATIONS

To run for president, a candidate must

- ★ be at least 35 years old
- ★ be a citizen who was born in the United States
- ★ have lived in the United States for 14 years

TERM OF OFFICE

A president's term of office is four years.
No president can stay in office for more than two terms.

ELECTION DATE

The presidential election takes place every four years on the first Tuesday of November.

INAUGURATION DATE

Presidents are inaugurated on January 20.

OATH OF OFFICE

I do solemnly swear I will faithfully execute the office of the President of the United States and will to the best of my ability preserve, protect, and defend the Constitution of the United States.

WRITE A LETTER TO THE PRESIDENT

One of the best things about being a U.S. citizen is that Americans get to participate in their government. They can speak out if they feel government leaders aren't doing their jobs. They can also praise leaders who are going the extra mile. Do you have something you'd like the president to do? Should the president worry more about the environment and encourage people to recycle? Should the government spend more money on our schools? You can write a letter to the president to say how you feel!

> 1600 Pennsylvania Avenue
> Washington, D.C. 20500
> You can even send an e-mail to: president@whitehouse.gov

BOOKS

Aller, Susan Bivin. *Ulysses S. Grant*. Minneapolis: Lerner Publications, 2005.

Editors of Time-Life Books. *War between Brothers*. Alexandria, VA: Time-Life Books, 1996.

Hakim, Joy. *Reconstruction and Reform*. New York: Oxford University Press, 2003.

Hakim, Joy. *War, Terrible War*. New York: Oxford University Press, 2003.

Larkin, Tanya. *What was Cooking in Julia Grant's White House?* New York: PowerKids Press, 2001.

Patrick, Bethanne Kelly. *Ulysses S. Grant*. Philadelphia: Mason Crest Publishers, 2003.

VIDEOS

American Experience: Ulysses S. Grant, Warrior President. DVD (Alexandria VA: PBS Home Video, 2002).

The American President. DVD, VHS (Alexandria, VA: PBS Home Video, 2000).

The History Channel Presents The Presidents. DVD (New York: A & E Home Video, 2005).

National Geographic's Inside the White House. DVD (Washington, D.C.: National Geographic Video, 2003).

INTERNET SITES

Visit our Web page for lots of links about Ulysses S. Grant and other U.S. presidents:

http://www.childsworld.com/links

Note to Parents, Teachers, and Librarians: We routinely verify our Web links to make sure they are safe, active sites—so encourage your readers to check them out!

INDEX